CW00348521

Intr

The town of Wimborne Minster derives its name from the river which runs through it and from its principal church, the Minster. The River Winburn, now known as the Allen, flows from the north and reaches the River Stour on the southern edge of the town. The Stour is the largest river in Dorset; it runs for over 70 miles from its source at Stourhead before reaching the sea at Christchurch. It was on the narrow piece of land between the two rivers that Wimborne Minster grew up and gradually expanded.

There are more than a dozen bridges within the town boundary, most of them over the Allen, but there are two major crossings of the Stour as it skirts the town, Julians Bridge to the west and Canford Bridge to the south.

Seven of the eight pointed arches of Julians Bridge. Originally a packhorse bridge of 1636, it was enlarged in the nineteenth century and triangular refuges for pedestrians were built into the parapets on either side.

Early History

In 43 AD the Roman army landed in Dorset at Hamworthy, near Poole, and soon established a base camp at Lake, half a mile to the west of the present town of Wimborne Minster. The invaders subjugated the local tribes, capturing the Iron Age hillfort at Badbury Rings, and setting up a system of Roman roads, using Badbury as its centre. Little is known of the next 650 years, although it is suggested that there was a gradual migration from Badbury to the more favoured position at Wimborne near the river crossings.

Wimborne's known history starts in about 705 AD when it was chosen by Ine, King of the West Saxons, as the site for the monastery for his sister, Cuthburga. The monastery had both male and female houses, possibly sharing the same church but living totally separate lives. Cuthburga, the first Abbess, had considerable power as head of the double community, which

Badbury Rings, a conspicuous landmark on the northern side of the Wimborne to Blandford road. Constructed around 500 BC, this Iron Age hillfort with three defensive lines of ramparts and ditches is crowned with a clump of trees. After the Roman invasion of 43 AD, and the defeat of the local Celtic tribes, the Romans took over the fort and it became an important staging post at the junction of Roman roads between Old Sarum and Dorchester, Bath and the port of Hamworthy.

Looking west from the ramparts of the Iron Age hillfort at Badbury Rings. The cattle grazing its slopes are the famous Red Devons traditionally bred at Kingston Lacy.

was the largest monastery in Wessex. At its peak, there were as many as 500 nuns here and it was a centre for much missionary work, especially in Germany. The shrine of St Cuthburga in the Abbey Church was an important place of pilgrimage in Saxon England. After the abbey had been destroyed by the Danes, it was refounded by Edward the Confessor, in the middle of the eleventh century, as a non-monastic body.

In Saxon times only the area in the immediate vicinity of the monastery was occupied; in the eleventh century the town was still clustered closely round the church. Medieval expansion took the town eastwards to the River Allen and southwards to the watermeadows of the River Stour. However, in the mid-fourteenth century, the Black Death wiped out the southern part of the town; the abandoned streets and house foundations can just be discerned as bumps in a grassy field called the Leaze to the south of King Street.

The shape of the present town had largely been established by the sixteenth century, although there was some expansion northwards in the eighteenth century, with fine Georgian buildings in East and West Borough.

Close by the Minster in King Street is St Joseph's, the oldest building still in domestic use. Of sixteenth century origin, it has a half timbered gable and an original first floor window.

Around the Town

The medieval pattern of narrow streets and alleys near the Minster Church still remains. Church Street leads directly to the north door of the Minster; Cook Row is a reminder of the importance of ready-cooked food in medieval life. The principal space is the Cornmarket, with buildings enclosing it on all four sides. Markets were held in this square from at least 1224, when the Dean of Wimborne's weekly market and St Cuthburga's annual Fair were transferred from their original venue in the churchyard. The markets and fairs were abolished in 1876, as a result of a public petition about rowdiness, but their modern equivalent, the Wimborne Folk Festival, uses the space effectively during the celebrations each June.

On the north side of the Cornmarket is the former Oddfellows Hall, erected in 1758 by the town's Friendly Society, and now the Heritage Centre. It originally had open arcades on the ground floor, and on the first floor is a large room with a

Dancers in the Cornmarket during the town's annual Folk Festival. First held about 20 years ago, the festival has steadily grown in size. It now features groups from all over the country, as well as hosting special visits of groups from such countries as France, Turkey and Germany. For a whole weekend in early June, the streets are closed to traffic and the town is alive with dancers and musicians, performing in the open air.

Palladian window overlooking the Cornmarket. On the south side was the George Inn, first recorded in 1524. The White Hart, a seventeenth century pub, stands on the west side. It is a timber-framed building, and its low doorway with a step down inside demonstrates how the street level has risen over the years. The town's stocks, now in the Priest's House Museum, were situated in the Cornmarket, and offenders were secured by the Parish Constable to a post inside the White Hart while they awaited their turn for punishment in the stocks.

The main Square of the town is a much later creation. In medieval times, St Peter's Church stood here. It later fell into decay, although in 1638 the derelict churchyard was used to bury over 400 victims of the plague. By the early nineteenth century, the church was in ruins, despite attempts to use it as a town hall. It was taken down, and the site cleared to provide a large open space. However, reminders of the graveyard still occur from time to time when the tarmac surface has to be dug up to service the drains, gas or electricity, and bones are unwittingly uncovered by the diggers.

The buildings around the Square are grander and larger than those of the Cornmarket. Banks and other such businesses predominate. On the west side is the King's Head Hotel, an

The Minster Tower is a good vantage point for a comprehensive view of the town. In the foreground is the Minster Green with the medieval Cook Row facing it. Just visible in the bottom left is the former Oddfellows Hall in the Cornmarket, with a Palladian first floor window; to the right, the Priest's House and the High Street which leads to the Square. In the distance, leading from the Square is West Borough, with open countryside beyond.

In the maze of narrow medieval streets round the Minster are interesting small buildings like the Oddfellows Arms in Church Street.

Looking down the High Street from the Square. On the left are early 18th century shops and the Albion inn with its coaching arch; the buildings on the right are mostly late 18th century.

eighteenth century coaching inn, its façade reconstructed after a fire in the 1880s. Another important coaching inn, the Crown, stood on the site now occupied by Barclays Bank.

The King's Head and the Albion in the High Street are a reminder of Wimborne's past as a coaching station. Horse-drawn coaches travelled daily to Salisbury, London, Plymouth, Bath and Portsmouth, and there was stabling in the town for perhaps 100 horses. The trade declined with the advent of the railway, but these two inns retain their large coaching arches through which the vehicles would pass to reach the stabling at the rear.

In the eighteenth century, expansion of the town took place mostly to the north, where the wider streets of East Borough and West Borough contain some of Wimborne's finest buildings. Just off the Square, in East Borough, is Percy House with a five bay front; next door comes Dormers, now a pub and restaurant, with a grand porch and a rear garden stretching to the River Allen. Opposite is East Borough Cottage, a small Regency house. Further on is Allendale House, with a large Doric porch, in whose grounds the Allendale Community Centre was built in the 1970s. The Workhouse, demolished in the 1950s, was also a feature of East Borough for some 200 years.

The charm of West Borough lies in its variety of scale, with quite small houses existing side by side with many more grandiose ones. The Conservative Club is a distinguished late eighteenth century house of three storeys, formerly the home of a family of Wimborne bankers. The Tivoli Theatre, which itself dates from the 1930s, occupies perhaps the finest Georgian building, the former Borough House. The Town Hall, in a building of 1830, has a large room on the first floor with an interesting plaster ceiling. Next to it is a pair of thatched cottages, which might have been demolished long ago, had not

Distinguished eighteenth century houses in West Borough.

ABOVE *Lewens, one of the most elegant of Wimborne's smaller houses, parts of which date from the seventeenth century.*

RIGHT *The former Wimborne Club in West Borough.*

the money run out for expansion of the hall. Nearby is Gulliver's House, where the infamous Dorset smuggler, Isaac Gulliver, made his home in his later law-abiding years, when he became not only a respectable citizen of Wimborne but also churchwarden of the Minster.

The heyday of smuggling was from the middle of the eighteenth century to the middle of the nineteenth century. High import duties made it profitable to smuggle tea, tobacco, silk, wool, wines and spirits from Holland, France and the Channel Islands. The excise men had a duty to keep watch on the inland routes, and in Wimborne their headquarters were in the King's Arms Inn in East Street. From the first floor window they would have had a good view of Eastbrook Bridge, which was the only crossing of the River Allen for traffic into the town from the east and south.

Eighteenth century Wimborne was an important centre of communications. Turnpike roads ran to Poole and Cranborne, Ringwood and Blandford, and eventually, in the 1840s, a turnpike was constructed westwards to the county town of Dorchester. Eastbrook Bridge, the old entrance to the town from the east had to be widened by 8 feet (2.5m) when the turnpike roads were constructed. It has a curious handrail consisting of upturned arrows, and a metal plaque with an alarming warning of the dangers of standing on the bridge!

Then came the railway. The Southampton & Dorchester railway opened in 1847, and by 1875 Wimborne Station was the most important junction in Dorset, with lines in five different directions. A substantial 'new town' grew up in the neighbourhood of the station, small villas with gardens and a new

Probably the last vestige of Wimborne's railway stands on the southern bank of the River Stour. The archway over what is now a public footpath from Wimborne to Canford was built by the Guest Family of Canford Manor to carry the railway line over their private carriageway. Sir John Guest was a shareholder in the railway company and, as an ironmaster from South Wales, had supplied the rails. The track from Wimborne station crossed the Stour nearby, but the river bridge has long since gone.

The monumental archway, built in a Tudor style of pale brick and stone, is covered with monograms and heraldic devices connected with the Guest family and topped with four pinnacles.

King's Court (1982), one of the small courtyard developments in the town centre, with ground floor shops and a first floor restaurant.

church, St John's. It was the fashionable part of town and even attracted the Dorset author Thomas Hardy for a few years in the 1880s. As the railway grew, the turnpikes declined, until at the end of the nineteenth century, all turnpike gates were removed and roads became the responsibility of the new County Council. In the twentieth century, the railway also declined in the face of increasing road usage. The passenger service continued until 1963, and the line was eventually closed in 1977. In 1981, part of the redundant railway land was used for a new road, the Wimborne by-pass, which relieved the town centre of much unnecessary traffic.

Twentieth century development in the town has been mostly to the north on fields which became accessible when new roads were constructed. A shopping centre was built in the 1980s on vacant land on an island in the River Allen. But more attractive have been the small courtyard developments on infill sites in the town centre, which have preserved the scale of the medieval town.

The Minster Church

The south side of the Minster, with its 'twin' towers.

The Minster stands on the site of St Cuthburga's Abbey Church. Begun in the eleventh century, rebuilding continued in the twelfth and thirteenth centuries. The interior shows the progression of the building. A spacious Norman nave, with massive arches, leads to the later chancel, in the Early English style. The centre lancet of the great East window contains fifteenth century Flemish glass. Underneath the chancel is the crypt which dates from the mid-fourteenth century and was, surprisingly, constructed after the chancel was complete.

The Norman pillars and arches of the nave lead to the crossing under the central tower, with the chancel and east window beyond.

ABOVE *The Astronomical Clock.*

BELOW *The Crypt.*

The western tower was added in the fifteenth century to house the bells, after it was realised that the Norman central tower was not strong enough to carry them. At that time, the central tower had a spire, said to rival that of Salisbury Cathedral. When the spire collapsed in 1600, it was never replaced, but the tower was capped to match the top of the west tower. It is these two 'twin' towers which make Wimborne Minster's outline unique and instantly recognisable.

High up on the north side of the west tower is a small wooden figure, the Quarter Jack, who strikes the quarter hours on his two bells. He is painted in the uniform of a Grenadier of the time of the Napoleonic Wars, although when installed in 1612 he was depicted in a monk's habit. On the south side is a rare type of free-standing sundial of 1676 with three sides facing east, south and west to catch the sun in all its positions.

A close look both outside and inside the church will reveal a wealth of small details. The central tower is decorated with intersecting arches, elaborately carved corbels and gargoyles on the corners. Inside there are carvings of heads both over the nave arches and in the chancel, and many fine monuments, some of them hidden in dark corners. Most of the stained glass in the windows dates from the nineteenth century when Wimborne obtained the services of some fine craftsmen.

In the Baptistry under the west tower is an Astronomical Clock of around 1320. Pre-dating Copernicus, its dial has the earth fixed at the centre with the sun, moon and stars revolving round it. The clock case is later, probably late sixteenth or seventeenth century, and the elaborately carved and gilded

The Chained Library.

cherubs and angels were added later still, having been at one time part of the organ case.

A narrow spiral staircase in the south choir aisle leads to the Chained Library, founded three hundred years ago for the free use of the citizens of Wimborne. It contains some 350 books, not all ecclesiastical by any means. Most of them are attached to the shelves by chains to prevent the citizens taking them away. The chains, of an unusual figure-of-eight design, were made in the town, probably by the children of the workhouse.

The Priest's House

Perhaps the oldest domestic building in the town, the Priest's House is thought to have been one of the houses occupied by the priests of the Minster. Parts of it date from around the early sixteenth century, and it was built in a U-shape with an open forecourt facing the street. In the eighteenth century it was extended at the front by filling in the forecourt space, but the original stone outer wall can still be seen internally at the rear of the front room. Stone is

Two views of the interior of the Priest's House Museum.

TOP *The Victorian Kitchen with its late nineteenth century range is in regular use for cookery demonstrations.*

RIGHT *The tinsmith's workshop in the Rural Gallery, used in the nineteenth and early twentieth centuries for repairing domestic utensils.*

an unusual material in Wimborne, the predominant building material in the town being brick.

The house was used for nearly two centuries for a variety of trades, a cloth merchant, a printer, bookseller and tobacconist and an ironmonger, and was much altered during this time with the development of shop fronts along the High Street. It became the Priest's House Museum in 1962, and was extensively restored in 1990. At that time, the street frontage was restored to its eighteenth century appearance. Inside are small rooms, reflecting the building's original domestic use; one of the rooms has a fine early seventeenth century plaster ceiling with a decorative frieze.

To the rear is the garden, the only one of many such High Street gardens to have survived in its original form. It is long and thin, stretching to the river, and is enclosed by brick walls.

The Priest's House garden, with its central path, is tended by volunteers who keep it in award-winning order.

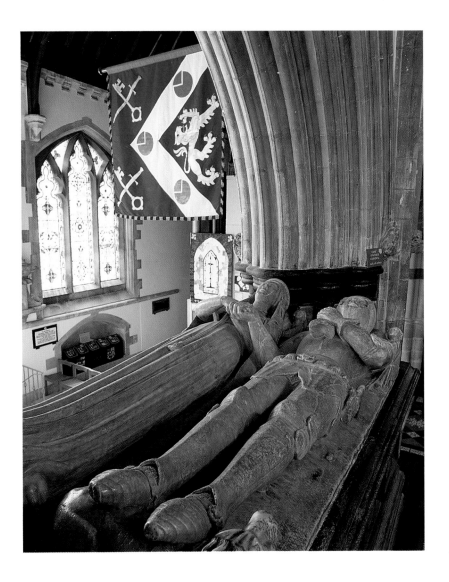

The tomb of John Beaufort, 1st Duke of Somerset, and his wife, Margaret, is one of the finest monuments in the Minster. It stands on the south side of the chancel, near the site of the chantry founded by Lady Margaret Beaufort in their memory.

Queen Elizabeth's Grammar School

Just south of the Minster is the former Queen Elizabeth's Grammar School, now converted to houses. The origin of the school was the foundation in 1497 of a chantry in Wimborne Minster by Lady Margaret Beaufort, mother of Henry VII. Lady Margaret was probably born locally at Kingston Lacy, her parents' home at the time, and after their death she set up the chantry with a priest to pray for their souls. She left instructions that the chantry priest should also teach Latin and Greek grammar. When the chantries were suppressed in 1548, it was recommended that this teaching should continue and in 1563 the school was granted a charter by Elizabeth I, Lady Margaret's great granddaughter.

A major rebuilding of the school took place between 1849 and

1851 to provide living accommodation for the headmaster, staff members and 50 boarding pupils. It continued to take boarders until just after the Second World War and admitted girls for the first time in 1953. The school became comprehensive in the early 1970s and moved to larger premises just outside the town. The attractive Victorian building has since been adapted for residential use and the nine houses there each bear the name of one of the former headmasters.

The fine façade of Queen Elizabeth's Grammar School is strewn with niches and gargoyles and has two charming ogee-capped turrets. Built of red brick and Bath stone, its homely mock-Tudor style commemorates the founder, Lady Margaret Beaufort.

Deans Court

Near where the River Allen joins the Stour, on the southern edge of the town, lie the house and grounds of Deans Court. Originally part of the monastic lands, the estate came to John Hanham in 1548 when the College of Canons in Wimborne was dissolved, and it has belonged to the Hanham family ever since.

The present house dates mainly from 1725, although internally the core of the medieval house remains, and there have been Victorian and more recent additions. It is surrounded by 13 acres (5.5 hectares) of woodland and grass, with some remarkably fine trees. Peacocks and other ornamental birds roam wild in the grounds. An organic kitchen garden is enclosed by an unusual Serpentine wall and contains a vegetable sanctuary, where rare varieties are being grown to save them from extinction. The large monastic fishpond, which once supplied the religious community with fresh food during the winter, lies south-east of the house.

Deans Court from the south, during the biennial exhibition of sculpture in the garden. On the right is the main building of 1725; the tall gable in the centre is a Victorian replacement of part of the medieval building; and on the left the modern kitchen wing can just be seen. The sculpture in the foreground is by Tim Harrisson.

Canford Manor

To the east of Wimborne, just below the ridge at Colehill, was the ford over the Stour known as Cana's Ford, and it was here on the south bank of the river that Canford Manor was built. At its most powerful, the Canford estate comprised all the land south of the Stour and had control of the harbour at Poole.

The earliest part of the manor still standing is the fifteenth century chamber known as John o' Gaunt's Kitchen, with its vast chimney breasts and fireplaces. For a long time the estate was owned by John o' Gaunt's descendants, the Beauforts, and at the end of the fifteenth century it was in the possession of Lady Margaret Beaufort, who founded the Grammar School in Wimborne. It is perhaps appropriate that the manor now houses Canford School.

Much of the medieval house had been taken down by 1825, and the core of the present house was built between 1825 and

The façade of Canford Manor from the south. The main building of around 1830 is in the centre with the later west wing to the left. Between them is Charles Barry's Gothic tower and hall, and to the right, under a red tiled roof, John o' Gaunt's kitchen.

1831. Later when the estate was owned by the Guest family, the architect Charles Barry (who was working on the Houses of Parliament) changed the building from a small country house into a grand mansion in the fashionable gothic style, with a tower and a medieval style great hall. The west wing of 1888 provided smoking and billiard rooms and private accommodation for the use of the Prince of Wales.

The school has occupied the house and immediate grounds since 1923, and has put up other buildings such as classrooms, boarding houses, a theatre, and a concert hall. But the grand manor is still there in its glorious parkland setting with many fine trees, and the Victorian 'medieval Gothic' hall continues in daily use as the school's dining room.

The village of Canford Magna, a model village built by the philanthropic Guest family to house the tenants of the estate, contains a number of cottages in a distinctive style with rustic porches, and also some earlier Georgian houses. The church is much older, the chancel being formed from the nave of an earlier Saxon church. The present nave and an unusually sited north tower were added in the twelfth century; there have been further additions over the centuries, and there are many interesting monuments.

Canford Magna village.

Kingston Lacy House and Estate

Kingston Lacy House was bequeathed to the National Trust in 1981 by Ralph Bankes whose family had lived there for over 300 years.

His ancestor, Sir John Bankes, bought both the Kingston Lacy and Corfe Castle Estates in the early seventeenth century and made his family home in Corfe Castle, which is between Wareham and the coast. He rose to become Chief Justice under Charles I, and remained loyal to the king during the Civil War. His home at Corfe Castle was besieged by the parliamentarians and, despite a heroic stand by his wife Mary, the castle was eventually taken and destroyed.

After the Restoration, his son and heir decided to build a new house on the Kingston Lacy Estate near the site of an earlier manor house. His architect, Sir Roger Pratt, was later one of the three Commissioners for the rebuilding of London after the Great Fire of 1666, and Kingston Lacy is the last remaining example of his work.

In the early nineteenth century, the young Charles Barry, architect of the Houses of Parliament, made extensive alterations to the house to accommodate a collection of works of art which William John Bankes had brought back from his travels in Spain, Italy, Greece, Egypt and the Middle East. It was William's enthusiasm and flair, his lifetime's passion for collecting, that converted this Dorset manor house into a treasure-house of art; the collection of Spanish paintings, for example, is only surpassed in this country by the Queen's collection at Buckingham Palace.

South-east of the house is the village of Pamphill, whose village green is cut by a fine avenue of oaks, planted in 1846 and leading to St Stephen's Church. On one side of the green is an elegant eighteenth century manor house and the cricket ground, on the other side the school and almshouses. The village inn and pretty thatched cottages lie below the green. The long range of Almshouses on the green was built in 1698 at the bequest of Roger Gillingham of the Middle Temple who was born in Pamphill. In the middle was a school room with accommodation for the schoolmaster over it and on each side were four almshouses, men on one side, women on the other. Twice a day, the schoolmaster was obliged to read a chapter of the New Testament to both the school and the almshouse residents.

Kingston Lacy House.

To the west of Pamphill is Cowgrove, a picturesque hamlet with seventeenth and eighteenth century thatched cottages and small farmhouses by the village pond. Other houses are earlier, dating from the fifteenth century, and there is a very impressive sixteenth century Court House.

In 1835, the year he inherited the Kingston Lacy estate, William John Bankes planted an avenue of beech trees along what is now the B3082 road between Wimborne and Blandford. It is said that originally there were 365 trees along one side and 366 on the other, one for each day of the year (or leap year), but some have now died and there has been replanting. Nevertheless, the avenue is more than 2 miles (3km) long and the trees are wonderful at any time of the year, being particularly spectacular in autumn.

LEFT *The thatched post office building in Hillbutts, to the north of Pamphill.*

FAR LEFT *The approach to St Stephen's Church (1907).*

BELOW LEFT *The east window in the church with the three Bankes children. The young Ralph Bankes sits on Christ's lap; Ralph's sisters, Viola and Daphne, stand by his side.*

RIGHT *Roger Gillingham's Almshouses on Pamphill Green, now occupied by the local village school.*

BELOW *The renowned Beech Avenue that lines two miles of the road between Wimborne and Blandford.*

The village pond at Cowgrove .

St Margaret's Almshouses

About half a mile north-west of Wimborne town centre, on the outskirts of the town, are St Margaret's Almshouses. Established around 1240 as 'sheltered housing', isolated from the rest of the community, for those with leprosy and other infectious diseases, they had become almshouses by the sixteenth century. The older houses are mostly thatched single-storeyed cottages, arranged round an informal courtyard. There are more recent houses in the garden at the rear. The Chapel of St Margaret and St Anthony, parts of which date back to the thirteenth century, served the leper hospital and, later, the almshouses; it is still in occasional use.

Thatched almshouses with the former leper chapel on the right.

The Model Town

Wimborne's Model Town is a one-tenth scale model of the town centre built between 1949 and 1956, and shows the shops and other buildings as they were at that time. Inside the model Minster a wedding is taking place, the Quarter-Jack on the tower strikes the bells and, in Park Lane, an old red telephone box, complete with buttons A and B, rings from time to time. Originally sited just west of the Cornmarket, the model was moved in the late 1980s to its present site in King Street where it has had scope to expand. It now has beautifully landscaped gardens, a model railway and fairground and a miniature town, a one-twentieth scale model of the model town.

The Model Town.

*In the Square of the Model Town,
children investigate the entrance to the
King's Head Hotel.*

Walford Mill

Walford Mill, on the northern edge of the town, stands on an island between the River Allen and the mill-stream. The water mill was one of several within the town boundary and is shown on a map of 1614. It remained in use as a corn mill until the mid 1960s although, around a century ago, the waterwheels were replaced by turbines.

The buildings now standing date from the late eighteenth century to the 1980s, when Walford Mill Craft Centre took over the site. Across the millstream is the former mill owner's house, also from the eighteenth century.

From the island there is a fine view of the seven arches of Walford Bridge. Originally a seventeenth century pack-horse bridge, this now carries the main road to Cranborne over the River Allen. On the south-west corner a metal plate still warns the owners of 'locomotive engines and other ponderous carriages' that the bridge is 'insufficient to carry weights beyond the ordinary traffic of the district'.

Walford Mill Craft Centre, with the old mill building on the left.

Wimborne Life

On the banks of the River Allen is the Allendale Centre, a community centre built in the 1970s. It is a meeting place for local groups and societies, and on Friday mornings houses a lively W.I. market.

Said to be one of the largest in southern England, Wimborne Market operates on Fridays, Saturdays and Sundays. As well as the traditional outdoor market stalls, there is a large and varied indoor market.

There have been markets in Wimborne since at least the thirteenth century. The Dean of Wimborne's weekly market originally took place in the churchyard and a rival market, set up by the lords of Kingston Lacy, was held in the area of East and West Borough. Later, markets were held in the Square and High Street, pigs were sold in the Cornmarket and there were butchers' stalls under the Oddfellows Hall.

The origin of today's market, on the eastern edge of the town, is a private cattle market established in the late nineteenth century in a field near the railway station. Cattle are no longer sold there, but there is a lively auction of poultry and game each year just before Christmas.

Bowling at Redcotts Recreation Ground. Redcotts field was given to the town in about 1910, and in addition to bowling, there are facilities for tennis, football, skateboarding and boules and also a playground for young children.

Country comes to Town. It is always a pleasure in summer to see a cricket match in progress in the middle of the town, across the river from the Crown Mead shopping area.

Christmas celebrations include a Steam Organ in the Square, Victorian events in the shops and museum and a children's procession through the town.

The text for this portrait of Wimborne was written by BARBARA WILLIS, author of several small guides and town trails about Wimborne, and who for many years worked in the Tourist Information Centre.

The photographs were specially taken by ROGER HOLMAN, an award-winning local photographer, well-known in Wimborne for his audio-visual presentations and whose work has regularly been exhibited in the town.